GW00402087

THE
Archive Photographs
SERIES

EPSOM AND EWELL

Race traffic returning from Epsom Downs on Derby Day passing the Spread Eagle, Epsom in about 1905. The taxi nearest the camera has crates of beer on its roof.

THE
Archive Photographs
SERIES

EPSOM AND EWELL

Compiled by
Richard Essen

THE
CHALFORD
PRESS

BATH • AUGUSTA • RENNES

First published 1994
Copyright © Richard Essen, 1994

Alan Sutton Limited
12 Riverside Court
Bath BA2 3DZ

ISBN 0 7524 00111 4

Typesetting and origination by
Alan Sutton Limited
Printed in Great Britain by
Redwood Books, Trowbridge

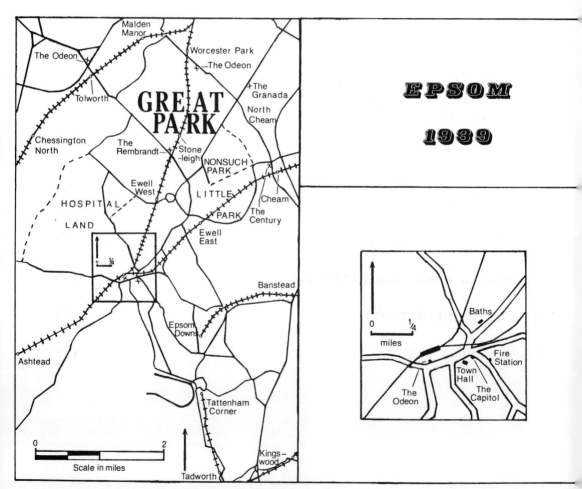

A map based upon the 1974 & 1987 Ordnance Survey 1:50,000 map with the permission of the Controller of H.M.S.O. (c) Crown Copyright.

Contents

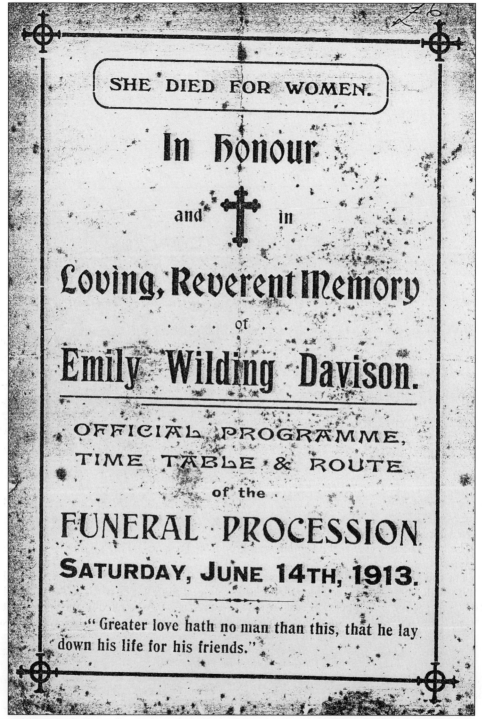

SHE DIED FOR WOMEN.

In Honour

and ✝ in

Loving, Reverent Memory

of

Emily Wilding Davison.

OFFICIAL PROGRAMME,
TIME TABLE & ROUTE

of the

FUNERAL PROCESSION

SATURDAY, JUNE 14TH, 1913.

"Greater love hath no man than this, that he lay down his life for his friends."

Emily Davison's Funeral card marking her demonstration against a Liberal Government. Epsom was such an establishment centre that it became a target for protest when Emily Davison the suffragette was killed after she threw herself in front of the King's horse Anmer during the Derby on 4th June 1913.

Introduction

Epsom and Ewell has a royal association which makes its history so much richer than surrounding boroughs. The racecourse had become part of the royal social calendar by the late 19th century and was at its most popular when 5 'lunatic asylums' were built on the other side of Epsom. They were used in both world wars when Epsom's Downs were selected as ideal training grounds. These were left isolated in fields until thirties housebuilding engulfed them, a process which was broken by the Second World War and finally finished in the fifties and sixties. This history is reflected in the 6 chapters of this book covering, the Edwardian Racecourse and Asylums (1899–1913), the First World War (1914–19), Between the wars (1919–39), the Second World War (1939–45) and the Post war (1945–95). Also the pictures in this book cover the period from 1895 to 1995 and mostly show views within the 1937 Epsom and Ewell borough boundaries.

The racecourse with its royal patronage is shown in Chapter 1. It not only attracted up to 1 million visitors to the races but also attracted other wealthy and powerful figures to live on the Downs such as Lord Rosebery which helped to shape the town. The desire to be near the racecourse and such people meant that the houses got smaller and more densely packed as you moved away from it towards the town.

The larger houses such as the Durdans and Woodcote Park had all been built on Chalk Lane and Woodcote in the mid 18th century. Lord Rosebery was attracted to this royal centre and bought the Durdans in 1874 and became the Liberal Prime Minister 1894–95, winning the Derby while he was in office. The middle classes followed the building of the railways in 1847, 1859 and 1865 allowing London businessmen to commute. This resulted in the building of a school the Royal Medical Benevolent College (1855) and villas on Worple Road, Ashley Road and St Martin's Avenue. The working class housing was furthest away from the course and between the tracks at East Street which linked Epsom with Ewell. Ewell did not have the same number of large houses as Epsom but was more influenced by links with the old royal palace of Nonsuch built by Henry VIII in 1538. This resulted in the mock castle design of the mansion built on the site of the palace being copied in Ewell at Ewell Castle and the Dairy.

Chapter 2 on the asylums shows them shaping Epsom in a similar way that the racecourse had done. The asylums arrived in much secrecy in 1889 when the Trotters sold the Horton estate to London County Council for the building of asylums. However they were not only to house lunatics but pauper lunatics which added to the social stigma. This may have become widely known as by 1896 the royal stables had moved from Epsom to Newmarket. The

4 asylums built in 9 years, Horton Manor (1899), Horton (1901), St Ebba's Epileptic Colony (1902) and Long Grove (1903–07) are all shown.

The pictures show the result of the new asylums with expansion on Hook Road, in the town itself and Epsom Common. Along Hook Road which linked Epsom to the asylums a small community was created of houses and shops with a school (1907) and St Barnabas church (1909). In Epsom itself at the gateway of Hook Road into Epsom social centres and businesses thrived. The Electric and Cinema Royal (1910) two cinemas were built either side of the entrance to Hook Road. On the aptly named Church Street the Congregational Church (1904), Baptist Church (1907) and St Martin's Church extension (1909) were built. Finally an Edwardian shop terrace (1896–1901), Grand Parade was constructed near one of Epsom's two stations. At Epsom Common a similar kind of community was created around Christchurch and a Mission Hall (1908) was built.

In Chapter 3 the First World War meant that the Downs were chosen as training camps including Woodcote park Camp and the Asylums were requisitioned as War Hospitals. The life of Woodcote Camp is covered from the arrival of the Universities and Public Schools Brigade in Epsom in 1914 to the riot which lead to the closure of the camp in 1919.

In Chapter 4 between the wars the pictures can be split between those of the twenties and thirties. The twenties pictures show the growth in recreational pursuits by a newly enfranchised middle class while those of the thirties show the farms and fields being replaced by their new houses. The First World War had been a shock and in reaction an escapist twenties society sought new forms of mass entertainment. In Epsom cycling, tea gardens and cinemas gave way to cars and buses, sport and supercinemas. Also the Grandstand was rebuilt and the white fascia of the shops and supercinemas became ideal backdrops for the corporate logo to promote shopping or viewing as a leisure activity.

During the twenties the granting of the vote to more women meant that the home became a political issue. This is reflected in the 'thirties pictures which show the housebuilding that replaced the farms at Epsom, Ewell and Stoneleigh. Epsom town centre grew in response as an administrative centre to this new electorate. This was confirmed by the creation of The Borough of Epsom and Ewell in 1937 and a series of high profile public buildings as an expression of civic pride. These included the Town Hall (1934), the Quadrant Parade of shops (1934), a fire station (1937), The Odeon (1937), the High Street widening (1938) and the Municipal Swimming Baths (1939). These were all built in red brick so as not to be confused with the white fascia of private businesses.

In the Second World War Epsom and Ewell had its own civil defences as a protection from the bombing and doodlebugs. Also land was brought back into use for farming at Epsom Common and Woodcote Park. In Chapter 5 on the Second World War a unique set of pictures shows Land girls farming on the golf courses at Woodcote Park. Some pictures of the golf course in the 'thirties have been included to show how much it had changed.

The last chapter looks at Post War Epsom recovering from the war in the late forties and early fifties which were known as the austerity years since food rationing ended very late in 1952. After post-war building restrictions were lifted the building work which had begun in the late thirties could be finished. The pictures show that the High Street widening was not completed until the late fifties! The last photographs show The King's Head and The Granada Cinema awaiting demolition and so in the last few views the Epsom of the sixties becomes more recognisable as the Epsom of today.

Richard Essen
November 1994

One
Edwardian
(1899–1913)

THE MOST POPULAR RACE TO-DAY IS **EPSOM!**

BATH

Racecourse

This seaside cartoon of c. 1930 provides a good introduction to Epsom famous for both its salts and the races. Epsom was a spa town in the late 17th century and its waters contained the laxative qualities of magnesium sulphate.

Horse drawn buses pass through Ewell High Street c. 1905. The first bus usually operates from Liverpool Street but on Derby Day is operating between Brixton Station and Epsom Downs.

Race traffic in Epsom High Street c. 1909 going to the races with a horse-drawn shuttle to Epsom Downs waiting on the left. Andrews the stationer is on the corner and The Spread Eagle, a local landmark on the other.

Race traffic on Downs Road, Epsom c. 1913 which was the steepest of the roads going up the hill to the course.

Arrivals to the Epsom racecourse on Derby Day lead by a 4 horse coach team c. 1905 on the opposite side to the Grandstands. Gypsy caravans can be seen behind the horses heads and behind them is the Prince's Stand of 1879.

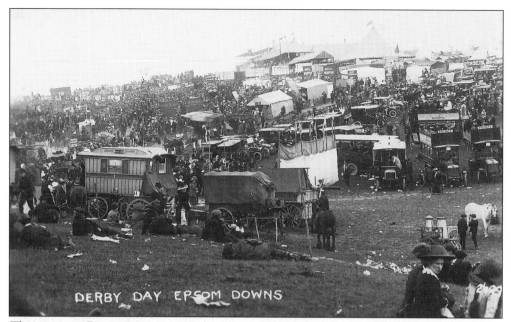

The scene on Epsom Downs on Derby Day c. 1912 with a view on the opposite side of the course to the Grandstand of privately hired B type General buses, a Sussex tourist coach, taxis, Gypsy caravans, tea tents, bookmakers and racegoers.

The Epsom Grandstand on Derby Day c. 1912 with a view taken the same day as the picture above. The Grandstand of 1827 with the royal box under the flag is surrounded by some of the 1 million raceday crowd.

Epsom Downs Station in 1907 with the Royal train and its coat of arms on the far left as you look at the picture. The station had 9 platforms and was opened by the London, Brighton and South Coast Railway for the race traffic in 1865.

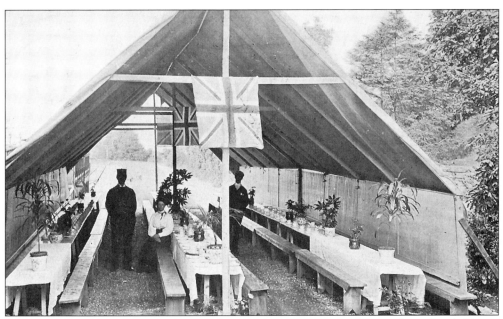

King Edward VII's Tent on Platform 9 of Epsom Downs station c. 1904 is adorned with Union Jacks. There was also a croquet lawn laid out on this platform by the aptly named Mr Sparks, the stationmaster.

The "Daily Mirror"

Mr Sparks in April 1914, the stationmaster for the London, Brighton and South Coast Railway's Epsom Downs Station 1900–14 posing on his retirement for which he got a silver cup displayed by Riddick the jewellers in Epsom.

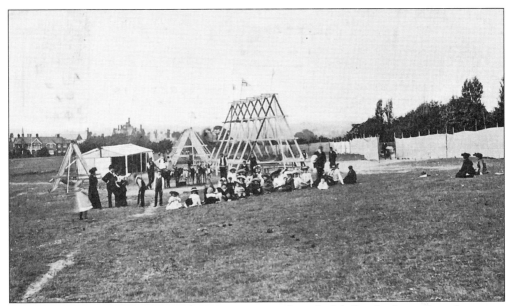

Epsom Downs Station c. 1904 with a merry-go round run by Mr Sparks. It was his job to raise the royal standard on Derby Day and to make sure that the King's coach was drawn up before his arrival.

The swings outside Epsom Downs station c. 1904 were hired by Mr Sparks who rented 500 acres from the Epsom Grand Stand Association and hired a fair to entertain children on Sunday school outings.

Lord Rosebery was Primeminister for the Liberal Party 1894–95 and his horse The Ladas won the Derby while he was in office and gave its name to the pub at the end of Chalk Lane. A previous owner of Durdans, Sir Gilbert Heathcote had also given his name to a pub on Chalk Lane with his Derby winner of 1838, Amato.

The Derby with its royal patronage was such an attraction for Lord Rosebery that he bought Durdans in 1874 and added an indoor riding school (1881) and stables (1900) to the estate. He won the Derby with The Ladas (1894), Sir Visto (1895) and Cicero (1905). The Durdans is shown here c. 1912.

Lord Rosebery's Garden Party and tea tables c. 1900 which sometimes hosted the royal party on their visits to Epsom. A row of female servants await the guests.

A gift of a water trough to Epsom from Lord Rosebery placed outside the walls of Durdans on Chalk Lane to celebrate his third Derby winner Cicero in 1905. It now stands outside the Rubbing House on Epsom Downs.

Chalk Lane c. 1912 showing the walls around the Durdans which were a feature of the large houses in Epsom built on the slopes of the Downs to enjoy the views and proximity to a royal social centre.

Alexandra Park, Epsom in 1909 with a team of girl Maypole dancers.

Rosebery Park presented to Epsom in 1913 by Lord Rosebery with the now demolished Summer House behind the trees.

Dorking Road, Epsom c. 1913 had large houses although it also lead to the Epsom Union Workhouse. Also Epsom's geology as a spring-line village is seen in the following views of the numerous ponds.

York House, Woodcote Green Road, Epsom, c. 1910 one of the many large houses built on the foot of the Downs to be near the course for wealthy landowners and London businessmen. It is now part of Epsom General Hospital.

Baron's Pond and Woodcote Park Lodge, Wilmerhatch Lane, Epsom c. 1913. Woodcote Park had been sold from John Trotter's Horton Manor estate in 1785 and bought by Mr Louis Teissier, a London merchant.

Woodcote Park House c. 1913 was sold by the Teissier family to the Brooks family in 1856 and onto the R.A.C. in 1911.

The Royal Medical Benevolent College c. 1903 on the slopes of the Downs near the course was opened by Prince Albert in 1855. It was renamed Epsom College in 1903 by which time the Earl of Rosebery was President of the College.

Wilson House, Epsom College 1901 was built by a donation from Sir Erasmus Wilson in 1873. Originally a boarding house under the direct supervision of the Headmaster, it was equated with the other houses of the house system in 1914.

The Biological Laboratory was built in 1886 since the College was founded for the orphaned sons of Doctors in a similar way that other middle class professions founded schools for themselves such as Wellington for soldiers and Christ's Hospital for clergy.

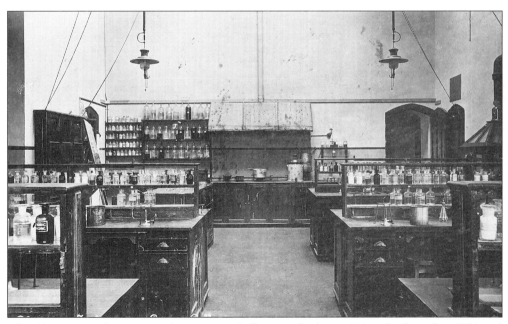

The Chemistry Laboratory c. 1900, Epsom College was built in 1871 and enlarged in 1901 and 1909. Although it and the biological laboratory had been installed earlier than most schools the curriculum was similar to other public schools.

The Cottage Hospital, Alexandra Road, Epsom was opened by HRH Princess Mary Adelaide, Duchess of Teck on 11th July 1889 as a memorial of Queen Victoria's Jubilee in 1887. It still provides medical services today as a Doctor's practice.

Church Street, Epsom c. 1900 was one of the network of roads including Ashley Road, Worple Road, Downside and St Martin's Avenue which was filled with middle class villas for those who could not afford a large house on the Downs.

Worple Road, Epsom c. 1900 with a milk cart delivering to the smaller Victorian villas. Worple Road ran from Church Street, cutting Ashley Road and continuing passed the walls of Woodcote Grove to reach Woodcote End.

Ashley Road, Epsom c. 1900 named after Mrs Ashley of Ashley House not only lead up to the Downs and the cemetery of 1871 but also to St Martin's Avenue which was known as 'Millionaire's Avenue'.

These 4 views are all of East Street which linked Epsom with Ewell. Polling Day in 1906 on East Street, Epsom outside the polling station front of the railway bridge shows a crowd awaiting the results. Aston's campaign office can be seen advertised on the shop front.

Waiting for the declaration of the poll on Polling Day January 1906 with a victory for the sitting Conservative MP William Keswick over the Liberal candidate Aston, supported by Lord Rosebery although nationally it was a Liberal landslide victory.

Mittendorf House, East Street, Epsom was donated to the National Incorporated Society for Waifs and Strays (Dr Barnardos Homes) by Miss Mittendorf. It was on the poorer side of Epsom well away from the racecourse and between the tracks.

The Locomotive, East Street, Epsom c. 1900 when it was a Free House run by the Proprietor P.C. Sharpe. It got its name from the nearby Epsom Town Station and until recently was called The Common Room.

High Street (formerly Greenman Street), Ewell with C.I. Curtis, the Ewell dairy on the left and The Green Man opposite. Further down the High Street is the Congregational Chapel demolished in 1938 and marked today by a small garden.

High Street, Ewell c. 1900 with the King William IV pub run by E. Smith offering stables and opposite the stationer Brunton which was taken over by E.H.J. Williams. In the middle of the picture is the London and Provincial Bank, later to become Barclays.

Church Street, Ewell c. 1902 with the grocer R. Bardrick advertising Schweppes drinks and a public telephone call office. Church Street used to be the main route to London but this was diverted to the new toll road, London Road in 1834.

The Old Watch House 1902. It was built c. 1790 and stored the fire engine which was needed with Ewell's timber-framed houses but was last used in 1869 and still survives today. The other door with the grills was used as a local jail.

The Spring Hotel on London Road, Ewell which was once a weather-boarded farm house but was well placed for the Derby traffic. It was said that the proprietor of the Spring Hotel could pay a year's rent from a good Derby week.

Spring Hotel, Ewell where the proprietor had Botanical gardens as an attraction in addition to catching the Derby race traffic. It was also said that King Edward VII when Prince of Wales had been held up for a quarter of an hour by the race traffic.

30

West Street, Ewell with the red brick National Schools building of 1861 on the right. The street met the London and South Western Railway's 1859 line to Epsom at an area called Gibraltar.

The Rectory House, Church Street, Ewell c. 1909 was the vicarage for St. Mary's Parish Church. Rectory House was designed by Henry Duesbury in 1839 and is older than the church built in 1848. It is now known as Glyn House.

Nonsuch Mansion built 1802–06 on the site of the Royal Palace of Nonsuch (1538) was built symmetrical with stucco walls and battlements and its influence is reflected on Ewell by the copying of its design at the Dairy (1810) and Ewell Castle (1810–14).

Ewell Dairy next to Bourne Hall was designed by H. Kitchen in 1810 and like Ewell Castle echoes the mock castle design found around Ewell but not at Epsom.

Asylums

A view from Horton Asylum Tower showing the asylum sitting in the fields with Hook Road surrounded by houses stretching off into Epsom.

"Thus the town remained rural and old fashioned. Now all that is changed . . .
A gaunt asylum shrouds the misery of hundreds of thousands of the mad patients of London"
(Gordon Home, 1901).

The Horton Manor and its estate, Epsom c. 1910 was bought by London County Council from the Trotters in secret. The House was incorporated into the Manor Asylum and Horton Asylum and the Epileptic Colony were built on the estate.

Middle Class Views on the Asylum

"From the midst of the foliage rises the great yellow brick tower of the Horton Lunatic Asylum, an unwelcome exchange for Horton Place the former seat of the Trotter family" (Gordon Home, 1901).

"A succession of meandering footpaths . . . have been seriously interfered with by the London County Council's mammoth lunatic asylum adjoining the tiny hamlet of Horton. The gaunt yellow brick walls and blue slate roofs seen through the trees are a cheerless sight, and one longs for the lusty creepers so seldom allowed to temper the external austerity of such institutions" (Gordon Home, 1901).

The Men's Quarters, Manor Asylum, Epsom c. 1907. It was the first of the Asylums and was built on the estate in 1899 for 2,100 patients in an L-shape.

St Ebba's Colony for the Epileptic Insane, Ewell c. 1907. It was the third institution to be built on the estate in 1902 when epilepsy was still considered as a mental illness. It was designed on the villa system for 366 patients by W.C Clifford-Smith.

Main Entrance, Horton Asylum, Epsom.

The main entrance of the 9th County of London Asylum Horton, Epsom c. 1907. It was the second of the asylums to be built on the estate in 1901 and was built in a crescent shape similar to the design of Bexley Asylum in Kent.

Administrative Offices, Horton Asylum, Epsom

The Administrative Offices, Horton Asylum, Epsom c. 1907 were needed in the running of an asylum for 2,100 patients with its own farm, chapel, mortuary and allotments as well as the wards.

Female acute wards, Horton Asylum, Epsom c. 1907. These 2 views show the division between men and women on the wards and the fact that the asylums treated both. Horton was built of yellow brick, a fact which inflamed writers in Epsom.

Male Infirmary ward, Horton Asylum, Epsom c. 1907 looking deserted although pavilions and seats are provided outside. The asylum was built on the fields of New Farm which it incorporated as Horton Asylum Farm.

Long Grove Asylum entrance gate, Epsom c. 1908 . It was decided that more accommodation was needed and a further 300 acres were bought to build a fourth asylum to be named Long Grove after the name of the estate.

The main entrance gate with the Administrative Offices behind of the 10th County of London Asylum, Long Grove on Horton Lane, Epsom c. 1908. It was built on the estate between 1903 and 1907 and could provide for 2,200 patients.

Long Grove Administrative Offices c. 1907 which formed part of the crescent shaped main building. During construction in 1905 a railway was built by the contractors Foster and Dicksee from Ewell West station to the building site to carry the building materials.

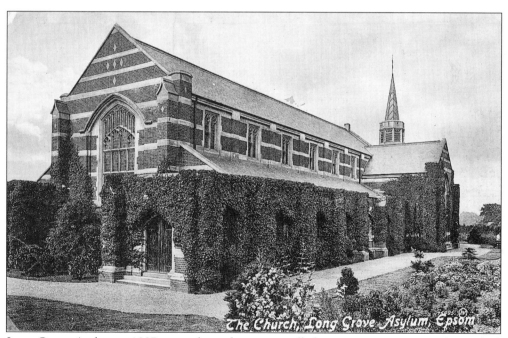

Long Grove Asylum c. 1907 was so large that it was called a town in miniature and even had its own church. It was built like Horton in a crescent shape but also using the villa system (the use of detached buildings) as at St Ebba's Epileptic Colony.

Hook Road, Epsom c. 1907 with the little corrugated iron chapel before St Barnabas church was built. The houses were for the new workers at the asylums who benefitted from their building.

Middle Class Views on Hook Road

"It is difficult to identify this with Hook Road of the present day, with its scores of houses, its own little church, and the extensive buildings of the Epileptic Colony, in connection with the already huge Horton Asylum of whose existence even we little dreamed twenty years ago or less" (James Andrews, 1903).

"Just where a pleasant lane, now known as the Hook Road (formerly Kingston Lane), leaves Epsom in a northerly direction, there has arisen a cluster of yellow brick, blue slated cottages, so that instead of passing straight from the town into open country, with picturesque honeysuckle laden hedges on either hand, which was possible four or five years ago, one must be content with an asphalt pavement and cast iron railings or uninteresting wooden fences for some distance. . . luxuriant hedges overgrown with honeysuckle are a priceless possession, and to unthinkingly destroy them is nothing less than criminal" (Gordon Home, 1901).

Skinner Brother's milk cart operating up East Street and Pound Lane. Milk churns were taken around on a pony and trap. The housewife brought her own jug to the churn and the milkman would fill his measure from the brass tap at the base of the churn and transfer milk to the jug.

St Barnabas choir outside the church in Epsom 1913 with a banner and a cross. The choir is mostly made up of men and boys and the vicar appears to be in the middle of the group.

St Barnabas church, Temple Road, Epsom 1909. It was a sub-parish of Christchurch but because of the estate of houses that was built on Hook Road, a new church was built and it became a parish in its own right.

Hook Road Council school c. 1907 on Pound Lane was built in 1907 to serve the children of the new residents of Hook Road, Upper and Lower Court Roads.

Epsom Congregational Church 1904. The arrival of 11,000 builders of the hospitals and resident employees meant that new social centres were needed and this was reflected in the building of churches for all the Christian denominations on the aptly named Church Street.

The Baptist Church on Church Street, Epsom was opened in 1907.

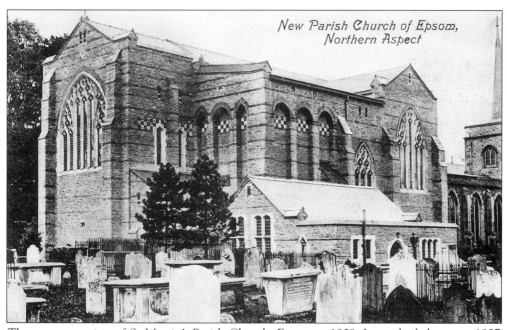

The new extension of St Martin's Parish Church, Epsom c. 1909. It was built between 1907 and 1909 as the first part of a cathedral and was needed for the more densely populated parish after the arrival of the hospitals.

The Cinema Royal and Electric Cinema opened in 1910 either side of Hook Road to capitalise on the potential new audience coming into the town between them. The shops next to the cinema include Boots, Eastman and Son and Elkin, a confectioner.

The Town Hall and Station Road (now Upper High Street), Epsom c. 1912. The Town Hall was more usually known as the Public Hall but when a new Town Hall opened in 1934 it was demolished and the Quadrant Parade of shops was built.

Church Street c. 1910 with J. Morgan's Dairy on the right and the Baptist Church of 1907 on the left. The large building behind the shops is the Technical Institute of 1895.

The narrow Epsom High Street c. 1912 with Norman's Stores, a hardware shop and C.W. Daniell the stationer on the right. A sign on the left directs people to the forge.

Gilbert Creasey's fish shop c. 1902 established in 1857 at the eastern end of Epsom High Street later became Tresize fish shop.

P.Nuthall's the Grocer, High Street, Epsom c. 1910 bought the shop from Ede's the baker and was situated opposite The Railway Inn on the junction of the High Street, Church Street and Station Road.

ESTABLISHED 1857.

Gilbert Creasey,

High Street, Epsom.

LICENSED DEALER IN GAME,

High Class Fishmonger and Poulterer.

Families waited on daily for Orders.

Telephone 31, Epsom.

Creasey's advert from a 1902 directory.

Epsom Town Station, c. 1912 opened by the London, Brighton and South Coast Railway was the first of the railways to arrive in Epsom in 1847. The station building still survives on Upper High Street today.

Station Road, Epsom c. 1910 with the railway terrace on the left and the Edwardian shop terrace (1896–1901) known as Grand Parade on the right. It was the Ashley Centre of the Edwardian era and Sainsburys had already arrived.

Epsom Station owned by the London and South Western Railway with its route to Waterloo opened in 1859. In comparison with Epsom Town the area around the station is a green field site.

The Clock Tower, Epsom c. 1910 at the quieter end of town. The Clock Tower was built in 1847. On the left the tallest building is the Post Office of 1897 which was part of a development on that corner and on the right is the King's Head.

The western end of Epsom c. 1910 was quieter than the eastern end. On the right is the Albion Hotel providing lunches, teas and accommodation for cyclists and Hersey's garage is on the left having expanded around the corner.

South Street, Epsom c. 1910. On the left is the Magpie Public House and on the right T. Hersey's earlier Garage advertising his services as a smith, farrier and general engineer. It later became the Woodcote Motor Services.

West Hill, Epsom c. 1910. Christ Church Hall is standing on a piece of ground donated by Mr G.H. Longman and opened in 1899 by Lord Rosebery.

West Hill, Epsom c. 1910 looking towards Epsom Common. Unlike the purpose built Hook Road there was no large scale building of working class housing along West Hill to the Manor Asylum only some middle class villas.

Old Waterloo House, Epsom c. 1910 is the first of the scenes showing the coaching revival at the turn of the century. The coach in front of it looks like The Rocket and has Ashtead and Mickleham on its sides as it turns up South Street.

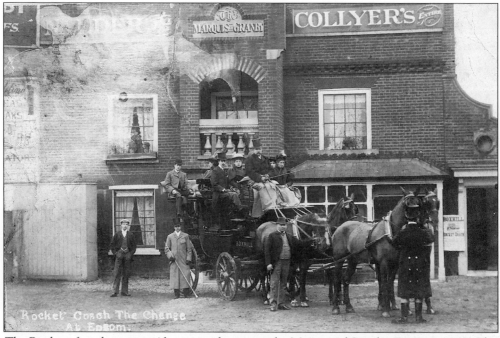

The Rocket after changing a 4 horse coach team at the Marquis of Granby, Epsom c. 1902. The destination names on the side read Leatherhead and Boxhill. The coaching tradition continued in the twenties when buses used it as a terminus.

54

The Venture at the King's Head Hotel in 1911 driven by Alfred G. Van der Bilt Most summer weekends it ran from London to Brighton.

West Hill, Epsom c. 1907 with a 4 horse team pulling what looks like The Venture passed Christchurch Hall and into Epsom.

Cottages on Epsom Common c. 1910. Epsom Common like Hook Road was an area near the asylums which expanded to provide new homes for the workers at the hospitals and jobs for those already living near the Common. The jobs not only included more variety for example as gardeners, kitchen staff, needlewomen, laundry and carpenters but also had higher wages.

Middle Class Views on Epsom Common

"From this part of the Common one looks down towards Christ Church and the cottages and pond of Stamford Green. The smallest of this little collection of dwellings is little more than a wooden cabin. . . From the pond the deep blue-green gorse of the Common forms the horizon to the west, but northwards the wooded acres of Horton Manor are marred by the tower of the new Asylum" (Gordon Home, 1901).

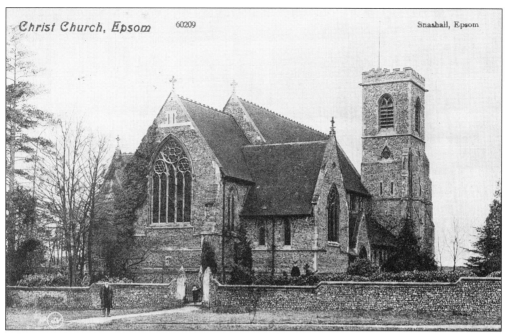

Christ Church, Epsom Common was consecrated in 1876. Lord Rosebery was a regular worshipper and later added the south aisle.

Stamford Pond, Epsom Common c. 1910 with the Working Men's Club in the middle of the photograph. The Epsom Common Mission Hall on Woodlands Road at the Wells was consecrated as a church in 1908.

The interior of Christ Church, Epsom Common c. 1910 showing the screen given in 1909 in memory of W.S. Trotter. It was here that the aristocrats of the racecourse and the asylums met since Lord Rosebery was a regular worshipper at Christ Church and The Manor Asylum was built opposite on the other side of Christ Church Road.

Two
First World War
(1914–19)

Grand Stand, Epsom Downs,

W.H.A 3385,

The Great War Stand on Epsom Downs is to the left of the main buildings. It was built in 1914 and almost straight away became the Epsom and Ewell War Hospital.

The Universities and Public School Brigade assembling in Epsom High Street on 17th September 1914 for billeting on Epsom, Ashtead and Leatherhead for 30 weeks.
They had selected the south-western part of Woodcote Park, Epsom for a camp.

The Public Schools Brigade on a traction engine of Stone & Co. Although the main contractor was Humphreys Ltd. of Knightsbridge, about 400 men of the Brigade some skilled in engineering, surveying and draughtsmanship were sent to work on the camp.

The 4th (later the 21st) Public Schools battalion building their huts at the new Woodcote Park Camp. The huts 120 ft. x 20 ft. were timber framed and lined internally with matchboarding (including the roof) and externally with corrugated iron.

Woodcote Park Farm Camp clustered among the trees in 1915 was occupied by the 18th battalion. It was part of an earlier plan to build a smaller camp but war office plans meant a second area had to be laid out for 5,400 men and 200 officers.

Lieutenant Colonel W. Wolridge Gordon of the 19th Battalion the Royal Fusiliers at Woodcote Park Camp on his horse. The Brigade was organised into 4 battalions (18th, 19th, 20th and 21st).

The 19th battalion Royal Fusiliers on parade at Woodcote park Camp, Epsom. Their huts were nearest the entrance to the Camp.

A Group photo of C company of the 20th battalion Royal Fusiliers in 1915 outside their hut at Woodcote Park Camp.

A kitchen at Woodcote Park Camp 1915. Each battalion had a cookhouse and canteen.

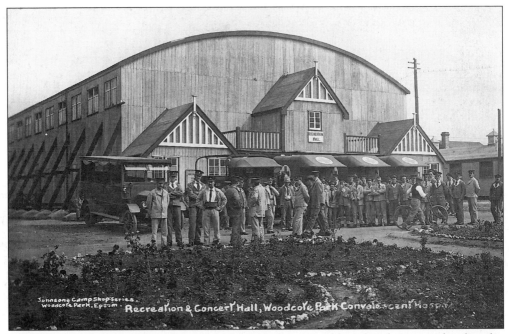

The Recreation Hall with ambulances and convalescent soldiers lined up outside after the Public Schools Brigade had left. Woodcote Park then became a convalescent hospital from May 1915 to August 1916.

The Woodcote Park Convalescent camp hairdressing saloon and Johnson's Post Office next to the Recreation Hall among the trees.

The Queen Mary Tea Rooms were one of the tea rooms in the hospital grounds where there was a lunch room, reading and writing room and a billiard room. It was opened by Queen Mary who gave her name to it.

A view of the main road through Woodcote Park Camp taken from outside the Recreation Hall. The ambulances are outside and opposite are the huts of B Division since the huts were labelled alphabetically. In the distance is the spire of the chapel.

The Manor (County of London) War Hospital entrance. At the outbreak of war 2 of the asylums, the Manor and Horton were taken over as war hospitals early in 1915 and the asylum patients were evacuated.

The Manor War Hospital tea room complete with palm trees and women serving tea and providing a good view of the blue uniforms of the convalescents.

The Horton County of London War Hospital Recreation Hall, Epsom where the large group of convalescents are waiting to be served with St Julien tobacco by the 3 women behind the table.

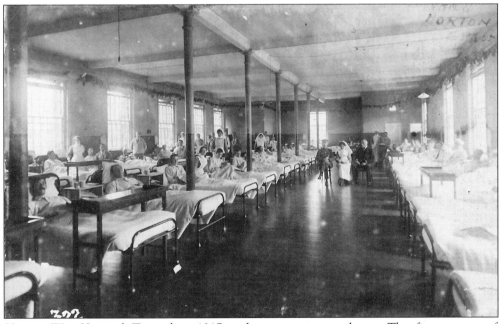

Horton War Hospital T ward c. 1917 with nurses in attendance. The first convoy of ambulances arrived on 20th May 1915, which was the first of 227 until it closed as a War Hospital in 1919.

INTERIOR Y.M.C.A. HUT AT CANADIAN CONVALESCENT HOSPITAL, EPSOM

The inside of the Canadian Y.M.C.A. hut, Woodcote Park. During August 1916 the Convalescent Hospital was handed over to Canadian Forces and in addition to the building of a Y.M.C.A. hut a baseball league was introduced from October 1916.

CANADIAN Y.M.C.A. HUT, WOODCOTE PK. EPSOM.

The outside of the Canadian convalescent hospital YMCA hut, Woodcote Park. The difficulty of keeping up to 3000 men on Epsom Downs was partly solved by providing entertainments.

Epsom Policemen outside Epsom Police station Ashley Road in 1919 including Inspector
Pawley sitting on the chair who was in charge of the police station at the time of the Epsom
Riot when Station Sergeant Green was killed (Metropolitan Police Museum).

Epsom Police station, Ashley Road on the morning of the riot on the 18th June 1919 after hundreds of Canadian soldiers from Woodcote Park camp had tried to release 2 soldiers arrested for disorderly behaviour at The Rifleman (Metropolitan Police Museum).

Ashley Road, Epsom on the 18th June 1919 showing how the fence outside was ripped up to throw at the police station to make missiles in 1919. The Police Station was demolished in 1963 and now Finachem House stands on the site (Metropolitan Police Museum).

Three
Between the Wars
(1919–39)

The War Memorial, Ashley Road Cemetery, c. 1922 was unveiled in December 1921 and a walled backgound with the names of the fallen was added in 1923 including gates dedicated to the Public Schools Brigade.

The Electric Theatre, East Street c. 1920. It became The Pavilion Theatre in 1926 and closed in 1929. The sign of The Rifleman pub can be seen on the left where the events leading to the Epsom Riot began.

The Picture Palladium on Station Road (now Upper High Street) c. 1920, home to Epsom Town Club. It opened in 1916 and closed in 1930.

Ivydene, South Street, Epsom, c. 1923 a place popular with Club cyclists now the Pizza Piazza. Large numbers cycled out from Wandsworth every Wednesday evening many on tandems. They drank ginger beer with milk called "speed".

The Roseary Tea Gardens, Epsom c. 1924. The entrance was on one of the shops next to Waterloo House. The building became a Wimpey Bar in the Seventies and is currently Kentucky Fried Chicken.

St Martin's Parish Church and Pagden's brewery, Church Street, Epsom before 1922 with the buildings of the brewery extending over half the forecourt of the parish church.

74

Church Street, Epsom.

Church Street, Epsom c. 1907 an earlier view which shows the Georgian houses which fronted the brewery. The tower of the Congregational Church can be seen poking over the tops of the houses.

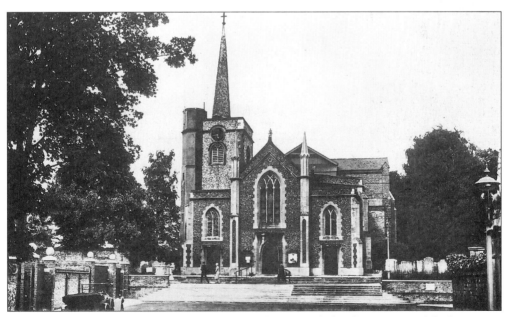

St Martin's 1922 after demolition of the brewery by W.T. Clark. The position of the brewery is revealed by the clean white steps which replaced it.

Ewell Motor Services c. 1920 on the High Street looking up Cheam Road with the Cave tea rooms next door and The Star Public House and Barclays Bank opposite.

Fields Garage, Dorking Road, Epsom is now a B.P. service station. The wall opposite belonged to Abele Grove which became a school run by the Convent of the Sacred Heart in 1923.

St Mary's Parish Church, London Road, Ewell with The General bus company's route No. 70 which from 1924 ran between Morden and Dorking via Ewell.

The Spring Hotel & Garage at the junction of London Road and Kingston Road c. 1923 which has changed from servicing coach and horses to servicing cars.

The 406 bus at Reigate Garage c. 1933. East Surrey buses first ran it from Epsom (Marquis of Granby) to Redhill as route S6 in 1920 and extended it to Ewell and Kingston in 1922, renumbering it 406 in 1924.

NS type bus Epsom High Street c. 1929 on General route no 164. The headboard reads Morden Station, St Helier Ave, High St Sutton, Sutton Lane, High Street Banstead, Epsom College, Station Road Epsom.

Reigate Road, Ewell c. 1929 with the Bypass 1931–32 not yet built. General route no 131 is on the Sunday summer only service which ran from Morden station via Reigate Road, Ewell and Longdown Lane to the Derby Arms at Epsom Downs 1928–30.

A Captain of the 1st St Martin's, Epsom Girl Guides 1918. The movement was started by Baden Powell, with his sister Agnes in 1910 for girls.

Garbrand Hall, Ewell c. 1920 home of the Torr family until 1896. House-building has already begun around the island but the house was saved from a similar fate when the name was changed to Bourne Hall and it became a school.

A junior class at Bourne Hall Private Girls School, Ewell c. 1926. It opened in 1925 but had a short life ending in 1953. In 1962 it was disgracefully demolished and in 1970 a modern circular building including the library replaced it.

The Park Keeper's House on the Court Recreation Ground, Epsom, c. 1929. The first part of the 21 acres was bought from Epsom Court Farm in 1924 and the last part in 1928. This was just one change of use of Epsom's Farms.

The cricket pavilion of the Court Recreation Ground under the oak trees c. 1929 which contained 2 cricket pitches, 2 football pitches, 2 hockey pitches, 2 hard and 3 grass tennis courts and a bowling green.

Rosebery Park 1930 with the Bandstand. During the summer band performances were given on Sunday and Wednesday evenings with the latter including programmes for dance music for dancing on the grass.

Rosebery Park, Epsom c. 1938 did not allow any organised games but children were allowed to sail their boats on the pond.

A rural Horton Lane, Epsom c. 1935. In 1928 East Surrey buses extended route 418 from Epsom toWest Ewell (Bungalow Stores) via Horton Lane and the hospitals in the Long Grove/Horton district.

The Manor Herd, Manor Hospital Park, Epsom c. 1920 was one of the hospital farms which included Horton Farm. The change of the name from lunatic asylums to mental hospitals happened after the First World War.

Manor Mental Hospital, Epsom c. 1930 with Horton Mental Hospital behind it. The different shapes of the hospitals can be seen with the L-shape of The Manor and the semi-circular shape of Horton. Around 1930 the population of the hospitals was a fifth of the population of Epsom and Ewell.

Hendon near Four Acre Wood on the Horton Light Railway in January 1938 with a train of 12 ton coal wagons to shunt to the Central Pumping Station which heated all the hospitals (Greater London Photography Library).

The Horton Light Railway

The Horton Light Railway inherited its track and rolling stock from the contractors railway built to carry the building materials between Ewell West station and Long Grove Asylum. When Long Grove Asylum was finished in 1907 the contractors Foster and Dicksee sold the line including the 2 engines Hollymoor and Crossness to the London County Council. In 1908 they drew up plans for a railway running from Ewell West station to Long Grove, the Central Pumping and Electric Light Works and the proposed hospital at West Park. It was built in 1913 and straight away carried coal to the boilers but the First World War delayed the building of West Park. At its peak in the twenties and thirties it carried 15,000 tonnes of coal a year. Crossness was sold in 1935 and replaced by Hendon which lasted until 1946 with the last engine Sherwood running until closure in 1950.

West Park Mental Hospital c. 1925 was begun in 1913 and the newly built Horton Light Railway delivered the building materials. Work stopped for the First World War so the last and fifth hospital was not finished until 1924.

West Park Hospital and stew ponds on Epsom Common c. 1935. The Hospital was named after 2 nearby farms West Farm and Park Farm.

Ewell West Station was built by the London and South Western Railway and is shown here in 1925 after electrification of the line from Epsom to Waterloo. Housebuilding followed at estates near the station

EPSOM URBAN DISTRICT COUNCIL
(ELECTRICITY DEPARTMENT)

= Electricity =
Cookery Demonstrations

will be held at

THE TECHNICAL INSTITUTE
Church Street - - - - Epsom

during the two weeks

June 13th to 18th *and* June 20th to 25th

3—4 p.m. and 7—8 p.m. each day

YOU ARE INVITED TO ATTEND

A publicity card for the Epsom Urban District Council's Electricity Cookery Demonstration at The Technical Institute, Church Street, Epsom.

Ewell East Station was built by the London, Brighton and South Coast Railway and was still served by a steam service as the line from Epsom to Victoria was not electrified until 1929. The tank engine is an ex-Brighton Class E5 No 593.

A Race special near Belmont heading for Epsom Downs Station behind Southern Railway Class I3. The 3rd rail is already in place after electrification of the line on 17th June 1928.

The New stand provides a backdrop to the people standing on top of their cars to get a bettter view of the race, 1931.

Gypsies c. 1938 and their painted horse-drawn caravans on Epsom Downs near Langley Vale in front of the 2 new stands built in 1927.

Tattenham Corner Station c. 1925 was built by the South Eastern and Chatham Railway making Epsom one of only 2 towns in Surrey served by 3 railway companies. Behind it are fields before the building of the Surrey Downs estate.

Tattenham Corner c. 1929 shows the dipping slope of the racecourse which was moved after Emily Davison threw herself at the King's horse in 1913. Behind it is the now vanished bull ring enclosure and on the far left is the station.

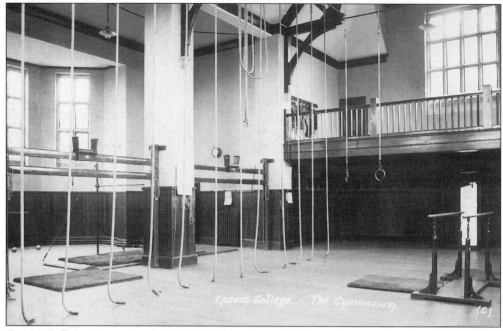

Epsom College Gymnasium built in 1909 has changed little and was similar when I went there except the gallery had gone.

Epsom College 1st XV season 1929/30 top left to right Griffiths, Keymer, Brisker, Gibson, Stewart, James, Hanbury, Moynagh. Bottom left to right Bowerman, Fox, Donby, Hodges (Captain), Kee, Watkins, Mc Ghie.

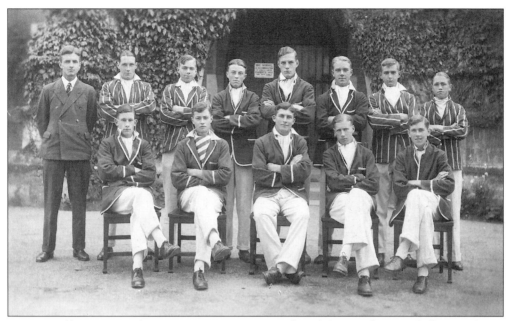

Epsom College 1st Cricket XI Summer 1928, standing left to right Mr Phillips, Holmes, Stunton, Bentleys, Pennington, Taylor, Younghusband, Caswell. Sitting left to right Robertsons, Bowerman, Rhys (Captain), Pettigrew, Hodges.

Epsom College Cricket Pavilion, 1927 was opened in the same year on Founder's Day by H.R.H. Prince Arthur Duke of Connaught who also presented the prizes.

An aerial view of the crossroads at Epsom 1925 with the newly built white Reids department store next to the stables of the Spread Eagle. On the far left is the now gone Wesleyan Chapel and on the far right the Court House.

Reids on Derby Day 1926. It was opened in 1907 by Mr H.L. Reid who owned a draper's shop at Surrey House on the High Street. In 1925 he was ready to make Reid's Corner Epsom's own department store.

The Capitol cinema, Church Street, Epsom, 1932 showing Harry Welchman in *Maid of the Mountains*. It was Epsom's first supercinema holding 1,513 people and a cafe and it was opened by Lord Ebbisham on 30 December 1929.

Boots, High Street, Epsom c. 1930 which had occupied this shop since before the First World War uses the white shop front as a backdrop for the corporate logo.

Epsom Town Station closed to passengers in 1929 but the goods yard remained open and Longhursts the builders took over the engine shed as a depot for building supplies c. 1930 (Lens of Sutton).

The Southern Railway passenger station opened in 1929 on the site of the London and South Western Railway's Epsom Station. It solved the problem of having 2 stations (Epsom and Epsom Town) with 2 goods yards controlled by 4 signal boxes within half a mile of each other (Lens of Sutton).

Westhill Avenue c. 1924 to be developed as The Chase Estate by H.H. and F. Roll on the fields of Epsom Court Farm. The arch is a similar idea to the one on the entrance of Briarwood Road, Stoneleigh Park.

Copse Edge Avenue near Epsom College built by Harry Roll in 1928 who also built houses on Horsley Close (1930–32), The Chase Estate (1930–32), Hookfield Road (1932–33) and Digdens Rise (1934–37).

The Research Department of Distillers Limited 1930 at The Great Burgh, Yew Tree Road built originally by Mr Colman of Nork Park on the edge of the Borough of Epsom and Ewell. Today it is Smithkline Beecham.

The Derby Arms opposite the Grandstand was supplied by the brewers Page and Overton who also supplied The Wellington in Epsom. It was the terminus of General route 131 for a brief period between 1928 and 1930.

The Drift Bridge Hotel as it was in 1933 having just been built at the junction of Reigate Road and Fir Tree Road next to the Drift Bridge Garage and Fir Tree restaurant.

The narrow Epsom High Street in 1920 before the High Street rebuilding began. Pullingers bought the corner store from Andrews in 1913.

Epsom High Street 1938. The first part of the High Street widening was completed 1934-38 and involved Scott and Serle demolishing and rebuilding up to the Railway Inn leaving it stranded in the middle of the High Street.

Epsom High Street in 1938 with Burtons and Boots already occupying the new Broadway of shops which was like the Ashley Centre of the thirties. Boots had moved out of the old corner site which was demolished by 1939 but not rebuilt until the fifties.

Epsom High Street 1939 with Lloyds Bank which replaced Pullingers on the corner of the High Street. Lloyds had begun building ahead of the widening and was forced to dismantle its building.

Epsom High Street Sunday 20th September 1925 before The Odeon was built with a milk delivery to W. Mash the confectioner, Elphick the butcher, The George Public House and R. Chamberlain's bakers shop.

Leatherhead Road, Epsom is actually South Street, a new block of shops has been built on the right replacing Hersey's Garage and Sebastian Lang the hairdresser has opened up on the left of the street. Compare with the photograph on page 52.

Epsom High Street with The Odeon, 1938. W. Mash's shop still sells confectionery, Elphick's has become Marshall's fish shop, The George has been rebuilt and The Odeon cinema has been built on R. Chamberlain's bakers shop.

Epsom High Street 1936, a policeman directs the traffic since traffic lights did not arrive until 1938. Dorset's hardware store and the Westminster Bank are on the corner.

Ruxley Lane, Ewell at the junction of Chessington Road c. 1920 surrounded by fields before housebuilding began and it looked like the view opposite.

Housebuilding in Ewell

Edwardian Ewell sat in a triangle of land between the 2 railway lines. Epsom's population had risen by a third between 1921 and 1931 to 27,089 but in comparison the population of Ewell only numbered 7,798 in 1931. The result was that farms were quickly bought up especially where the land was near the 2 railway stations (Ewell West and Ewell East). At West Ewell, Ruxley Farm and Ewell Court Farm were sold and the estates of Ewell Park, Ewell Court (1932–37), Ewell Court Farm (1932–37) and Ruxley (1936–37) were built. Further building was blocked by the hospital land. At Ewell East E.G. Harwood who built the Woodcote Green estate in Epsom also built 3 estates at The Higher Green (1930), Ewell Downs (1932) and The Green (1932). M.J. Gleeson built more modestly priced detached houses at Nonsuch (1936) and Nonsuch Court (1937-39). However Nonsuch Park acted like the hospital land at West Ewell and blocked any further building.

Ruxley Lane, Ewell c. 1927. In 1930 housebuilding meant East Surrey Buses further extended route 418 (Effingham–West Ewell) northwards via Ruxley Lane and Kingston Road where it met route 406 to terminate at Tolworth tram terminus.

Ruxley Lane, c. 1927. Surrey Motors was started as a garage business in Sutton by William Rees Jeffreys in 1919. Within a year the company had expanded into coach operation to the south coast resorts. A K2 telephone box is outside Ruxley Stores.

Hedgers Library, 10 Ruxley Parade, Kingston Road c. 1932 with a K2 type telephone box. The films advertised at the Capitol, Epsom were Maurice Chevalier in *The Playboy of Paris* and Richard Cooper in *Officer's Mess*.

Ruxley Parade c. 1950. Hedgers Library has become Ruxley corn and seed stores at the junction of Ruxley lane and Kingston Road

Chestnut Avenue, Ewell c. 1938 on the Davis Estate built 1934–37. The card is from Hedgers Library and the road is very near Ruxley Parade.

Rossmore, Heatherside Road, West Ewell, Easter Monday 1926. The older couple appear in Edwardian fashion whereas the younger women are in up to the minute twenties fashion.

Riverholme Drive, West Ewell is also off Chessington Road. It was part of an estate built 1931–33 next to Ewell West Station.

Lansdowne Road, West Ewell Bungalows c. 1930 also between Chessington Road and the Hogsmill stream.

Stoneleigh Park aerial view with Stoneleigh Station sitting amid the fields in 1932, Briarwood Road stretches across the fields to London Road and Nonsuch Park beyond. Soon mock Tudor houses will fill the Parks of a Tudor Palace (Epsom Stamp Company).

Stoneleigh

'Stoneleigh' was one name given to the massive development of part of 911 acres of the Great Park of Nonsuch. The whole area had been bought by the Landed Estate Company in 1865 but it was left to The Stoneleigh Estate Company to build on it south of Worcester Park. It bought up the fields of 3 farms (Coldharbour Farm, Sparrow Farm and Worcester Park Farm) in 4 years. It then auctioned 353 acres which were bought by property agents such as Atkinson Marler who bought up Stoneleigh Park estate (1932). The result was estates called Stoneleigh Hill (1933), Cuddington, Chesterfield Park, Davis and Tolworth Hall (1934–37).

Calverley Road, c. 1936 was part of the Stoneleigh Park estate. Notice the mini roundabout which were common on the estate and stopped buses running through it, making Stoneleigh dependent on the railway.

Briarwood Road, Stoneleigh c. 1936 after completion with brick arches at the entrance to Stoneleigh Park estate.

Ewell Court Parade, Kingston Road c. 1930 when it was still a single lane highway served by the 406 bus. The Rembrandt cinema was built opposite in October 1938 by Mrs Thompson who had sold The Cinema Royal, Epsom to build it.

The Organ Inn, London Road, Ewell c. 1930 was one of 2 mock Tudor superpubs built on London Road. C.W. Bromley, the proprietor was soon to benefit from the building of the Ewell Bypass in 1931.

PROPERTY

IN

EWELL, EPSOM, STONELEIGH
and District

SHOPS, INVESTMENTS, HOUSES, LAND, ETC.

Consult the Estate Agents:

PAUL & MILLS

203 KINGSTON ROAD
EWELL

Station:
STONELEIGH

Telephone:
1718 and 2413

A 1937 advert of Paul & Mills an estate agent on Kingston Road.

Nonsuch Park entrance c. 1920 which blocked further house building. It was a fare stage for General route no 70 Morden to Dorking via Epsom and Green Line buses Oxford Circus to Dorking.

Nonsuch Park's 260 acres c. 1920 were bought in 1937 by London County Council, Surrey County Council and the Boroughs of Sutton and Cheam and Epsom and Ewell and are now run by a joint management committee of the 2 boroughs.

Four
Second World War
(1939—45)

During the war the Royal Automobile Club was directed by the Surrey War Agricultural Committee to turn over some 110 acres of Woodcote Park to food production. The tractor shown here was often driven by a man and not a Land girl. The official reason for this was that the blackout had made many garage hands redundant.

Woodcote Park, Epsom c. 1936. An aerial view shows the golf course before it was ploughed up and the open-air swimming pool (on the far left) built in 1933.

Woodcote Park House, Epsom with a view of the red brick which replaced the stucco after a fire on 1st August 1934.

Woodcote Park House golf course under agriculture with the House in view on the far right. Wheat, barley, oats, potatoes, sainfoin and hay were grown and varied each year.

Woodcote Park House with the workers sitting out on the terrace near the ivy.

Bee-keeping at Woodcote Park. Despite these agrarian pursuits the Park did not escape bombing and one of the craters was turned into a bunker at the end of the war.

Poultry farming at Woodcote Park which also provided grazing land for Sheep. The Park was also used for training by the local Home Guard lead by Lieutenant Cuddiford and Sergeant Harry Roll and including members of the R.A.C..

Woodcote Park within the kitchen garden walls where fresh vegetables were grown even before the war.

Woodcote Park Land girls harvesting onions/potatos. The Women's Land Army was the only women's civil service directly under government control being under the honarary directorship of Lady Denman and 30 civil servants.

Land girls picking apples on ladders. The land was still not returned to the R.A.C. by 1947 when it was hoped it would be returned after the harvest. The Committee of the R.A.C. was making arrangements for the rebuilding of the new course to be available for play early in 1949.

Five

Post War

(1945—95)

A London Transport type STL bus at Epsom Racecourse operating a special service from Morden Station after racing was resumed. *Picture Post* was sold from 1938 to 1957 and covers most of the post war period in this chapter.

The Swail House Estate, Ashley Road was developed by the London Association for the Blind in 1952 (now Action for Blind People). Worple Lodge was converted and named after the benefactor Martha Swail and flats were added at the back.

Ewell High Street c. 1950. The chemist on the corner is run by Sydney Best and the King William IV pub is sponsored by Ind Coope and Allsop formed from a merger in 1934. Barclays Bank is still on the corner of Cheam Road and the High Street.

Epsom High Street c. 1948. On the right The Quadrant Parade of shops built in 1938 has replaced The Public Hall and a roundabout stands in front of the Home and Colonial.

An incomplete Epsom High Street c. 1948. New street lights now illuminate the widened High Street and a car park has been built behind Boots but the corner site where the Railway Inn stood has not been rebuilt yet.

The King's Head, Epsom High Street 1957 which was demolished in the same year by Charles Griffiths Limited of London (Mrs S. Quemby).

Schweppes

In the late 1940s and early 1950s Schweppes the drinks manufacturers began campaigns of innovative adverts. In 1950 Schweppshire, an imaginary English county, was invented by the firm's managing director and the humorist Stephen Potter over a game of snooker. The idea was developed and places in the county included Schwepping Forest, Schwepstow Castle (Queen Elizabeth schwept here) as well as Schwepsom Downs.

The Odeon, Epsom High Street 1957 showing The Happy Road. A Scout Parade lead by John Beckwith passes in front in Baden-Powell's centenary year and 50 years of scouting. Neon lighting has replaced the double-armed electric lamps (Mrs S. Quemby).

The Granada, Church Street, Epsom 1960. It used to be The Capitol but became The Granada in 1947 with its junior club of Granadiers. It closed during 1960 and briefly became a Keymarket and Waitrose before it was demolished. Capitol House now stands on the site preserving the name (Mrs S. Quemby).

The Clock Tower, Epsom   28063

Epsom High Street c. 1960. The King Shade Walk has replaced The King's Head Pub and is offering lock-up shops to rent. The Odeon still stands not demolished until 1974, Elys' sign is in the distance and a Mini is approaching.

Epsom High Street c. 1963 is finally complete as the corner is filled in with a building of matching neo-Georgian style into which Waitrose moved. Burtons is still in the same place in the High Street but Tescos has replaced Williamsons.

Epsom Downs Station on 5th June 1966 and the visit of a Southern Counties Touring Society rail tour 'The Surrey Rambler' behind Battle of Britain class no 34089 602 Squadron. The line is still worked by mechanical signals operated from Epsom Downs signal box which burnt down in a fire on 16th November 1981. The whole line was moved back in 1989, the station was demolished and a new one built. The area shown is now covered by a housing estate.

Acknowledgements

Acknowledgements are due to the Greater London Photography Library, the Epsom Stamp Company, Mr R. Lane, Lens of Sutton, the Metropolitan Police Museum, the Ordnance Survey and Mrs Shirley Quemby.

Books used include Gordon Home's 1901 Epsom, its history and surroundings, James Andrews' 1903 Reminiscences of Epsom, Cloudesley Willis' 1931 A short history of Ewell and Nonsuch, Living History Publication's 1976 Epsom Town, Downs and Common and 1981 Epsom Common, George Cockman and John Marshall's 1988 Old Views of Epsom Town and Richard Essen's 1991 Epsom's Hospital Railway, 1991 Epsom's Military Camp, 1992 Thirties Epsom and 1993 Epsom's Suffragette.